CW00482689

S.H.I.N.E

A Collection of Inspiring Messages to Strengthen. Heal. Ignite. Nourish and Edify **the** Soul

By

Eydie Robinson

S.H.I.N.E: A Collection of Inspiring Messages to Strengthen, Heal, Ignite, Nourish, and Edify the Soul

ISBN: 979-8-9856197-3-7 *(paperback)*
ISBN: 979-8-9856197-4-4 *(hardcover)*
ISBN: 979-8-9856197-5-1 *(eBook)*

Scripture quotations taken from The Holy Bible, New International Version® NIV®
Copyright © 1973 1978 1984 2011 by Biblica, Inc. TM
Used by permission. All rights reserved worldwide.
Scripture quotations are from the ESV® Bible (The Holy Bible, English Standard Version®), copyright © 2001 by Crossway, a publishing ministry of Good News Publishers. Used by permission. All rights reserved.
Scripture quotations marked KJV are taken from the King James Version. Public domain.
Scripture quotations marked NKJV are taken from the New King James Version®. Copyright © 1982 by Thomas Nelson. Used by permission. All rights reserved.

Cover design: Ground Floor Group
Cover photo: J Dionne Photography

Printed in the United States of America
Robinson Anderson Publishing
2150 South Central Expressway, Suite 200
McKinney, TX 75070
info@rapublishingco.com

To my grandmother and mother in heaven, I dedicate this book to you. It is not a day that goes by that I don't think about the both of you. I hope that I have made you proud!

To my children, Chris, Makayla, and Aubrey. You are my reason for working so hard; you keep me going. God definitely blessed me when he gave me the three of you... my own little personal angels. I love you!!

Table of Contents

PREFACE

I have gathered these messages God has given me over the. years, and I finally decided to put them in a book.

These messages have inspired me, given me hope, and reminded me how good God truly is. I hope they will do the same for you.

As you read through this book, I pray that you allow the words to sink in. Meditate on them and open your heart to hear what God is trying to say. Hopefully, through this, your relationship with God will strengthen.

There is no specific order to this book; just go to whatever you feel like you need on that day or at that given moment. However, I do believe it is important during your spiritual journey to discover who YOU are and how to find your identity in Christ. But after that, allow the messages to do what they are designed to do: Strengthen, Heal, Ignite, Nourish and Edify your soul.

Blessings!

Eydie Robinson

WHO ARE YOU?

Do You Know Who You Are? This may be one of life's most defining questions and for most, the answer is simple. However, let's look past the surface level answers that include the roles you play, what you do and who people want you to be. Rather, focus more on your identity through the lens of God and who he says you are.

I challenge you to look deep within yourself and find out! At times, we tend to have more negative thoughts about ourselves than we do positive ones. Now is the time to reverse them! Why? Because God wants you to experience His love. He wants you to know that as His son or daughter, you are more than you think you are! You are royalty and you are chosen. It is by no mistake that you are currently sitting at tables where on paper you aren't "qualified." It is also by no mistake that the visions and dreams you've had and the ideas you suddenly come up with are designed specifically for YOU! Release the negative thoughts and self-doubt and truly get to know who you are, in Christ. When you look in the mirror, look hard and take a minute to see yourself as God sees you! So, who are you?

📖 John 15:16 NIV

> *You did not choose me, but I chose you and appointed you so that you might go and bear fruit—fruit that will last—and so that whatever you ask in my name the father will give you.*

WHO AM I? HOW TO FIND YOUR IDENTITY IN CHRIST

- ⊙ Listen to your heart.
- ⊙ Get to know your feelings, thoughts, reactions, and actions.
- ⊙ Know why you do what you are doing. Become more aware and conscious.
- ⊙ Know the love you have inside yourself. When you can connect with this love, this will help identify who you really are.

"You are a chosen people, a royal priesthood, a holy nation, God's special possession, that you may declare the praises of Him who called you out of darkness into His wonderful light." (1 Peter 2:9, NIV)

"We are God's handiwork, created in Christ Jesus to do good works, which God prepared in advance for us to do." (Ephesians 2:10, NIV)

"See what great love the Father has lavished on us, that we should be called children of God! And that is what we are! The reason the world does not know us is that it did not know Him." (1 John 3:1, NIV)

"You are no longer foreigners and strangers, but fellow citizens with God's people and also members of his household." (Ephesians 2:19, NIV)

WHO AM I?

Scriptures to guide your thoughts...

2 Corinthians 5:17, **A new creation**

Ephesians 2:10, **God's handiwork**

Ephesians 1:4, **Chosen...holy & blameless in love**

Ephesians 1:5, **Predestined...for himself**

Ephesians 1:7, **Redeemed and forgiven**

Ephesians 1:13, **Sealed with the promised Holy Spirit**

Ephesians 2:4-5, 2:6, 2:10

STRENGTHEN

/ˈstreNG(k)THən/

make or become stronger (verb)

You Are a New Creature in Christ

When you accept Christ as your Lord and Savior, He forgives you, washes you, makes you clean, and you become "a new creature" in Him. The most exciting part is, when you walk in newness and accept that you are a son or daughter of the King, you are beginning a relationship that will develop more fully as you spend time getting to know who God is and who he says you are.

As you draw closer to Him, you will begin to see a change in your mindset, and even how you walk, and talk will be transformed. Not only that, your newness will be noticed by those around you. As you strengthen your relationship with Christ, you will see a transformation of the "old" while in pursuit of the "new". Your confidence will begin to develop as you come to know who you are in Christ. After all, with becoming a new creature in Christ, you are not who you were. You now have a royal legacy and access as an heir.

📖 **2 Corinthians 5:17 NIV**

> *Therefore, come out from them and be separate, says the Lord. Touch no unclean thing, and I will receive you.*

📕 **Scriptures to guide your thoughts...**

> *2 Corinthians 4:16, 2 Corinthians 10:4-5, Ephesians 4:23, Colossians 3:10, Romans 6:6, Romans 12:1-2, Galatians 2:20*

♪ Prayer

Gracious and heavenly Father, I am ready to walk in the newness you speak of. I am ready to be washed clean and I thank you for providing me the opportunity to do so. I love you Lord and I am ready to walk with my head held high in confidence knowing that I am your child. Amen.

Don't Give In

Being afraid does not mean that you are a coward. In fact, being afraid is a good indication of when you would need to rely on God, even more. His word clearly states that He did not give us the "spirit of fear; but of power, and love, and of a sound mind" (2 Timothy 1:7 KJV). So, if you are experiencing fear, don't give up on what you're doing, use the opportunity to lean in closer to God and ask him to show you how to proceed or execute (power), in a way that is pleasing to him (love) and to give you peace with what he has blessed you to do (sound mind). God knows the plan; you just have to execute it.

1 Corinthians 9:24 NIV

> *Do you not know that in a race all the runners run but only one gets the prize? Run in such a way as to get the prize.*

Scriptures to guide your thoughts...

Psalm 34:4-5, Matthew 8:25-27, Luke 1:12-14, Proverbs 3:23-24, Deuteronomy 31:6

Prayer

Lord, I thank you for already working things out in my favor. Allow me the strength to not give up and continue to fight. I will not give up Lord, I will not give up. Amen.

Your Divine Power Can Destroy Strongholds

Many of the lies that are in our heads have been there for awhile and are called "strongholds." What is even more disturbing about strongholds is the control they have on our personal lives as well as the detriment of being passed on to other generations. Strongholds can be present in our daily thoughts and actions; however, the Bible tells us that we have divine power to demolish them. So, exercise your power and get those negative thoughts out of your mind and actions by going to the Bible and studying the truth. [For example, if your stronghold is rejection, seek scriptures about God's acceptance.]

📖 Jeremiah 23:29 NIV

> *"Is not my word like fire," declares the Lord, "and like a hammer that breaks a rock in pieces?"*

🕮 Scriptures to guide your thoughts...

2 Corinthians 10:4, 1 Corinthians 10:13, Romans 12:2, Ephesians 6:12, 1 John 4:4

🕯 Prayer

Heavenly Father I come to you right now and ask you to demolish every stronghold and mind-oppressing spirit that is trying to keep me bound. I pray that every plan the enemy has for me will fail. I exercise my power and I thank you for strength right now in the name of Jesus!

Affirm Yourself!

Stop seeking validation from your peers, your family, and social media! Stop seeing other women and men as competition! Instead, empower one another! More importantly, empower yourself! Stop speaking lowly of yourself and putting negativity into the atmosphere, blocking opportunities that could propel you forward! You've got this! Affirming yourself through God's word and developing your true identity is monumental to strengthening your relationship with Christ. I challenge you to see yourself as God sees you; as royalty, worthy, called, capable, successful, prosperous, strong. Speak it, believe it and receive it!

📖 John 15:5 NIV

> *I am the vine; you are the branches. If you remain in me and I in you, you will bear much fruit; apart from me you can do nothing.*

📑 Scriptures to guide your thoughts...

1 Chronicles 16:11, Ephesians 6:10, Romans 15:13

🕯 Prayer

Lord, I pray right now that I will no longer seek validation from others. I will see myself as you see me. I am worthy, I am successful, and I am loved. In Jesus name. Amen

The Shift

The atmosphere is shifting, both in the natural and spirit realms. A shift brings about a change and, in many instances, when we think about change, it makes us feel uncomfortable. One comfort you have is knowing that as the atmosphere is shifting, God is forever the same. He is masterfully orchestrating the pieces of your life to make something beautiful. You may feel like you are standing alone, or you may even feel like you're in the wilderness but during this time you are building humility, strength, and character, so don't be afraid! Continue to seek God, trust, and have faith that he has a plan for your life.

📖 Psalm 34:4 NIV

> *I sought the Lord and he answered me; he delivered me from all my fears.*

📓 Scriptures to guide your thoughts...

> *Ecclesiastes 3:1, Hebrews 13:8, Isaiah 43:19, James 1:17, Jeremiah 29:11, Joshua 1:9*

🕯 Prayer

Lord, change is hard but one thing I know is that you do not change, and I thank you for that. I trust you Lord, and I trust that whatever shift you allow to take place in my life is for my good. Amen.

Worship is Necessary

Daily worship is required to strengthen your relationship with God. It is a time for you to shift your focus from the world; from yourself; and all other distractions, to commune with God. What is even better is that you can worship Him wherever you are. You do not have to go to a "special" place or wait until you go to church. You can meet God anywhere, at any time. How different do you think you would feel if you spent the first part of your day offering your worship unto God? How different would your life become if you increased your time of worship? What condition would the world be in if we all would worship God?

📖 Isaiah 25:1 NIV

> *Lord, you are my God;*
> *I will exalt you and praise your name,*
> *for in perfect faithfulness*
> *you have done wonderful things,*
> *things planned long ago.*

▓ Scriptures to guide your thoughts...

Exodus 23:25, Psalm 68: 4-5, Psalm 150:6, John 4:24

🕊 Prayer

Heavenly Father, I thank you! I give myself to you Lord God in worship and I praise your Holy name for you are worthy! Amen.

He Is with You

In times of trouble, He is there! When you lose confidence, He is there! When you are down, He is there! When it seems like trouble is coming from every direction, He is **STILL** there! The moral of the story is, God is always there! He promises never to leave you and to never abandon you. This is huge when you consider that His promise still holds true in situations that you may have brought onto yourself. Even when we walk away from him– He is still there! Trust and depend on Him, at all times; this means in good times and not so good times. He is a very present help! God is with you no matter what!

📖 Joshua 1:9 NIV

> *"Have I not commanded you? Be strong and courageous. Do not be frightened and do not be dismayed, for the Lord your God is with you wherever you go."*

📑 Scriptures to guide your thoughts...

Deuteronomy 31:6, Zephaniah 3:17, Revelation 3:20

🕯 Prayer

Lord, thank you for always being there even when I thought you weren't. Thank you for your protection, your guidance and your strength. Amen.

Encourage Yourself

It is important that we learn to be our own encouragement. Like the popular song says by Donald Lawrence, "Sometimes you have to encourage yourself, sometimes you have to speak victory during the test." When David and his men found themselves in hopeless situations, David didn't wait for someone to encourage him, he encouraged himself in the Lord. This is what you must do as a believer in God, and you must become good at doing so. When you know and believe in the promises of God, your confidence is strengthened. Not only are you showing God that you know who He is, but you are also acknowledging who you are in Christ. This pleases Him and allows Him to do His best work–through you.

📖 1 Samuel 30:6 NIV

> *"And David was greatly distressed because the men were talking of stoning him; each one was bitter in spirit because of his sons and daughters. But David found strength in the Lord his God.*

🎗 Scriptures to guide your thoughts...

1 Thessalonians 5:11, Psalm 121:1-2, 1 Corinthians 16:13, Romans 15:5

🕯 Prayer

Heavenly Father, I understand that sometimes I must be my own encouragement. However, sometimes it is hard. Help me Lord and allow me to be constantly reminded about what you have promised me. Amen.

You Are Called

Have you heard God's call? Do you have a desire or thought that frequently crosses your mind? Have you placed those desires on the back burner and feel that it's easier to continue with your current routine? Perhaps you've watched others seemingly work and flow in a task or position that is a natural fit for them and wondered, what God has called you to do?

Well, God has a specific purpose for each of our lives and you are called to use your gift(s) to serve others, according to His purpose. No one can fill the seat that God has reserved, specifically for you! So, get moving!!

📖 Philippians 2:13 NIV

> *For it is God who works in you to will and to act in order to fulfill his good purpose.*

📕 Scriptures to guide your thoughts...

Jeremiah 29:11

🕯 Prayer

Lord, thank you for the plan and the purpose you have for me and in due time I know that it will be revealed. I thank you and praise you *now* for what is to come! Amen.

The Choice is Yours!

There's a quote by Neil L. Anderson that says, "Faith and fear cannot coexist!" In all truthfulness, you may feel like your life experiences tell you otherwise. Although you may feel challenged with the choice between putting your faith over your fears, this is what God wants. Have comfort in knowing that God is gracious and understanding when it comes to your concerns. He has equipped you to move forward in faith, even in the presence of your fears. The Bible is clear that faith does not mature and strengthen without seasons of tests and trials, but he promises to be there with you, through it all. As you know, seasons do change! So, surrender your fears unto God and watch your tests and trials change to triumphs and testimonies!

📖 James 1:2-4 NIV

> *Consider it my pure joy, my brothers and sisters whenever you face trials of many kinds because you know that the testing of your faith produces perseverance. Let perseverance finish its work so that you may be mature and complete, not lacking anything.*

🏮 Scriptures to guide your thoughts...

Hebrews 13:6, Hebrews 11:1, Isaiah 41:10

🌱 Prayer

Heavenly Father, on this day I choose to let my faith overpower my fears and I thank you for always being with me even when it seems like you aren't. I surrender my fears to you oh God. Amen.

It Is Your Time!

This is your season!

Allow God to prepare you so that He can elevate you!

Prepare you for what? Elevate you to where? These questions may translate differently for others, but as a believer in Christ, you are to prepare for the time that you will be with Him. Take comfort in knowing that He has a divine plan and purpose for the time you spend on Earth. As you align your desires with those that He has destined for you, be diligent about pressing forward with what He has placed on your heart to do. How you spend your time and who you spend your time with are equally important. So until His appointed time…this is your time to make good use of the time He has given you. IT IS YOUR TIME!!!!

📖 Luke 12:35-38 NIV

> *Be dressed ready for service and keep your lamps burning like servants waiting for their master to return from a wedding banquet, so that when he comes and knocks, they can immediately open the door for him.*

📓 Scriptures to guide your thoughts...

Ecclesiastes 3:1, Micah 6:8, Colossians 3:23-24

🕊 Prayer

Precious and heavenly Father, I pray that I will be a good steward of my time by doing the things you have purposed and called me to do. In the mighty name of Jesus! Amen.

Stepping Into a New Season

As you move into each new season of life, there may be several questions formulating in your mind. Facing the "unknown" will prove to be a testing of your faith, but there is comfort in knowing that God knows what's next for you. The bible is clear that "there is nothing new under the sun" (Ecclesiastes 1:9,KJV), so in real-time we must remind ourselves daily that God has a plan and purpose for each of us. Similar to the changes that occur with climatic seasons, are actions that are common as we approach the new seasons of our lives. Most would agree that the process of change comes with some unfamiliarity, but there is certainty that as the process evolves, there is a transformation. "Old things are passed away" to make room for what is new (2 Corinthians 5:17, KJV). So, as you step into each new season of your life, know with certainty that God is in control of everything.

📖 **Daniel 2:21 NIV**

> *He changes times and seasons; he deposes kings and raises up others. He gives wisdom to the wise and knowledge to the discerning.*

📑 **Scriptures to guide your thoughts...**

Isaiah 43:18-19, Galatians 6:9, Ezekiel 34:26, 1 Thessalonians 5:1

🪶 **Prayer**

Lord, I pray that you continue to stand beside me as I walk into my new season. No longer am I afraid, In Jesus name, Amen.

When Attacked, Stay in Peace

O ne of the most used tactics by the enemy is frustration, and that frustration causes you to lose your peace. This is how he tries to control you; by getting you in a negative space. Don't let him win!

Peace in the midst of trials, tribulations and circumstances is what God has given you. Use it!

God will prepare a table for you in the presence of your enemies!! So, remember, when you are attacked, stay in a place of peace. Don't allow the enemy to win but *do* allow him to be defeated. He gets confused and doesn't know what to do when he can't get you upset.

📖 Psalm 37:8 NIV

> *Refrain from anger and turn from wrath; do not fret – it leads only to evil.*

🪧 Scriptures to guide your thoughts...

1 Corinthians 14:33, James 3:18, John 14:27, 2 Thessalonians 3:16

🙏 Prayer

Lord, thank you for your peace that surpasses all understanding. No longer will I allow the enemy to take me away from the beautiful place you have for me. I will not let him win! Amen.

Peace in God's Silence

Learn to have peace in God's silence and know that you cannot become anxious and start making your own decisions just because you don't hear Him. Stay on the path. Don't detour and try to take your own route. Silence does not equate to absence, and it doesn't mean that He doesn't care. Silence has many different meanings in different situations. Sometimes, it means that you are to keep doing what he has instructed you to do and other times it means that what you have asked for is not for you, or it's just not the right time. Trust Him and have faith. Don't move on your own accord. God has got you!

📖 Psalm 27:14 NIV

> *"Wait for the Lord; be strong and take heart and wait for the Lord.*

📑 Scriptures to guide your thoughts...

Romans 12:12, Psalm 27:14, 2 Peter 3:9, Isaiah 40:31, James 5:7-8

🕯 Prayer

Holy, gracious and heavenly Father. Continue to direct my path. Lead me and I will follow. I will no longer move on my own accord because I know that what you have for me is much greater than I can ever imagine. Amen.

Stay Focused

It is easy to lose focus during tough times and detour from our path of purpose. When we are struggling, it becomes easier than ever to compromise our actions or justify the decisions we make. However, as Christians, God does NOT want us to lean on our understanding; we are to choose His (Proverbs 3:5-6).

Take a step back and think about a time when you were going through a rough patch. Do you remember a point in time when things got worse? Did your actions align with seeking God's guidance before you took your next steps? When we defer to our ways, there is certainty that there will be a price to pay, and usually, that price in our peace. Now that you have been reminded of this, the next time you find yourself in a similar situation, don't forget to readjust your focus. Seek God's will for your next steps, stay focused on Him and remain in peace.

📖 Proverbs 4:25 NIV

> *Let your eyes look straight ahead; fix your gaze directly before you.*

📖 Scriptures to guide your thoughts...

Romans 8:5, 1 Peter 3:17, Matthew 24:13

🖊 Prayer

Heavenly Father, I ask for patience so that I don't make the wrong decisions. Lead me, guide me and help me to remember what is just and right. Amen.

Clean Out Your Closet

There comes a time in our lives when we have to "clean out our closets." This is not meant in literal terms but in the sense of getting rid of the clutter and disorganization that consumes our lives. Oftentimes, we have so many things on our minds and in our lives that need releasing before we can find peace. I ask you today, think about what you can release in your life that will free up space so you can experience the real peace of God.

📖 Isaiah 1:16 NIV

> *Wash and make yourselves clean. Take your evil deeds out of my sight; stop doing wrong.*

🔳 Scriptures to guide your thoughts...

1 Corinthians 6:19 - 20, Psalm 32:8, Proverbs 24:3-4

🙏 Prayer

Lord, help me identify the things in my life that need releasing so that you can dwell in me. Help me to declutter and give me the strength I need to let things go that are not of you. In the mighty name of Jesus, amen!

You Are More than a Conqueror

When you stand your ground by meditating on God's love and you learn His Word, you can beat the enemy down. Remember, you are more than a conqueror, you don't fight for victory, but you stand in the victory of Jesus. The Lord finished His work on the cross which assures us forgiveness, healing, peace, provision, protection, and acceptance of God. No attack, threat, lie, or accusation can steal these away!

📖 Zephaniah 3:17 NIV

> *The Lord your God is with you, the Mighty warrior who saves. He will take great delight in you; in his love he will no longer rebuke you but will rejoice over you with singing.*

▪ Scriptures to guide your thoughts...

Colossians 2:13-15, Romans, 8:37, 1 John 5:4, 1 Corinthians 15:57, Jeremiah 1:19

🕊 Prayer

Holy, gracious, and heavenly Father, thank you for being with me and thank you for reminding me that no devil in hell has power over me. I am a conqueror, and your Word is my weapon. Amen.

Take Off Your Mask

Oftentimes, we *"mask"* what is really going on in our lives. We put on a happy face and cover up how we truly feel. But in reality, we are depressed, hurt, fearful and angry. We portray the image of having it all together but behind closed doors we are suffering.

We cannot continue to live in that place! We must remove the mask and come to terms with our issues. We must get to the root of the problem and let God work. Are you ready to take off your mask?

📖 **1 Peter 5:7 NIV**

> *Cast all your anxiety on him because he cares for you.*

📖 **Scriptures to guide your thoughts...**

Psalm 91:14-15, 2 Samuel 22:33, 1 Peter 5:10, 2 Chronicles 20:4

🕊 **Prayer**

Lord, please give me the courage and the strength to remove any mask that either hinders me from experiencing true peace or that keeps me away from all you have for me. No longer will suffer in silence. Help me Lord!

Give Your Thoughts & Life to God

At times, we can become anxious in our thoughts *and* actions. When we become anxious it can distract us from our relationship with God and plunge our thoughts into darkness. However, we must give it to God. Philippians 4 tells us that when we pray and let our requests be known to God, he will give us peace which surpasses all understanding. We are to take comfort with this understanding which not only comes with peace to guard our hearts, but also to guard our minds, so give it to God! Fix your thoughts on God and His promises. He will help you!

📖 Proverbs 3:5-6 NIV

> *Trust in the Lord with all your heart and lean not on your own understanding; in all your ways submit to Him and he will make your paths straight.*

📓 Scriptures to guide your thoughts...

Colossians 3:2, Jeremiah 29:11, Romans 12:2

🕊 Prayer

Oh God, I pray against anything that distracts me away from you. Help me stay focused, Lord. Amen.

A Routine of Forgiveness

Take time to examine your life, often. If you're finding that there are things hurting you, more than helping you, it is time to let it go! Now, this is true for people, as well. Having a daily routine of forgiveness is monumental to moving on from hurtful experiences. Oftentimes when we think of forgiveness, the action involves someone who has wronged us. But take the time to digest that forgiveness is necessary for ourselves

(1 John 2:9). It is a very personal recognition and cleansing process that strengthens our relationship with God. Realize that He allows life's events to draw us closer to Him and to position us for His purpose. Now, I encourage you to strengthen your walk daily with His word, which will help you move to a place of peace and purpose.

📖 Hebrews 12:1 NIV

> *Therefore, since we are surrounded by such a great cloud of witnesses, let us throw off everything that hinders and the sin that so easily entangles. And let us run with perseverance the race marked out for us...*

■ Scriptures to guide your thoughts...

Matthew 16:14, 1 Peter 5:7, Ephesians 4:32

🕊 Prayer

Lord, I understand that forgiveness is not for the other person but for me and moving forward I intend to practice a routine of forgiveness. Amen.

Worry Not

Each day has enough trouble of its own.

Stop worrying and trust God! I know it is easier said than done, but many times we put so much energy in worrying about what "*could*" happen that we don't allow ourselves to enjoy what *is* happening. God wants us to keep our hearts and minds on Him (Isaiah 26:3). If we practice doing so, we are reliant on God for daily guidance; surrendering our will and trusting His. There is wisdom in knowing that worrying not only weakens your body, but also doesn't change what is going to happen. So, I encourage you today, to ask God for strength to trust Him and allow your mind and soul to receive His peace.

📖 Matthew 6:34 NIV

> *Therefore, do not worry about tomorrow, for tomorrow will worry about itself.*

📓 Scriptures to guide your thoughts...

1 Peter 3:4, Isaiah 35:4, Joshua 1:9, Psalm 34:4, Jeremiah 17:7-8

🪶 Prayer

Father God, today and moving forward I choose to enjoy what is happening now. My faith is in you Lord? Amen.

Cast Your Cares on Him

One of the many great things about our mighty God is that He allows us to release our worries upon Him. In the scripture below it says to cast our anxiety on Him because he cares for us, which means that we don't have to carry the burden. In fact, to "cast" something means to forcefully throw it out, or to get rid of (Merriam-Webster), so the intent is for us to no longer have it. All we have to do is to trust and have faith that God is bigger than our worries.

God's word says, in Matthew 11:28, when we come to Him he will give us rest, so stop stressing! Let's start anew by trusting God and remembering what He has already told us... Cast your cares on Him, He can handle it!

📖 1 Peter 5:7 NIV

> *Cast all your anxiety on him because He cares for you.*

🔲 Scriptures to guide your thoughts...

Psalm 55:22, John 16:334, Luke 12:25, Proverbs 12:25

🖋 Prayer

Father, thank you for carrying my burdens so I don't have to. Amen.

Love One Another

As Christians, it is important that we respect our relationships with each other and also love one another. We may not always agree but as God commands us, we must still show love to one another, and even to our enemies. This "new" command comes with a prescribed formula for us to use—which is to love, not how we potentially define love, but as God loves us. When you really think about the depth of God's love for you, despite your wrongs, you are sure to find that His formula for love has a better success rate.

So how do we show love? 1) Speak it and mean it. 2) Show it through meaningful and intentional actions. 3) Listen to understand and not to reply. 4) Affirm through positive words and encouragement.

📖 John 13:34 NIV

> *A new command I give you. Love one another as I have loved you. So, you must love one another.*

📓 Scriptures to guide your thoughts...

1 Peter 4:8, 1 John 4:11, Proverbs 10:12, 1 John 4:19, Matthew 5:43-48

🕯 Prayer

Heavenly Father, I pray that you fill my heart with the love that you so freely give so that I can genuinely show love to others. Thank you for your formula. In the mighty name of Jesus. Amen.

He Is Always Watching

There are unseen battles that God has conquered on your behalf, and you don't even know it. He has delivered you from tricks of the enemy on so many occasions that you would be shocked! He is protecting you, and to demonstrate how special you are to Him, He commands His angels to keep watch. How blessed are you that you have an entire army of angels concerned about your well-being, watching and guarding everywhere you go?

When Daniel was wrongfully thrown into jail, God sent His angel to shut the mouths of the lions, leaving Daniel unharmed. When you too are wrongfully accused, pray that God clamps the mouth shut of the very thing set out to destroy you. The omnipresent God always protects His children.

📖 **Psalm 121:8 NIV**

> *The Lord will watch over your coming and going both now and forevermore.*

🕯 **Scriptures to guide your thoughts...**

Genesis 28:15, Proverbs 15:3, Psalm 121:8

🕊 **Prayer**

Father God, I thank you for always watching over me and thank you for your army of angels that keep me safe. Lord, you are always there, and I am forever grateful. Amen.

The Puzzle Pieces of Life

Our lives are like a puzzle and each piece represents a part of God's plan and purpose for us. Surely, you would agree that when all the puzzle pieces are dumped out of the box, the puzzle looks more difficult to put together than when you first glanced at the picture on the box top. When the puzzle is under construction, sometimes the pieces fit together and sometimes they don't. This is also true in the journey of our lives.

When we come to a piece of the puzzle that doesn't fit in our lives, we must remember that there is a season and a time for everything. There are reasons for the "misfit"; perhaps the piece that doesn't fit may not be suited for you or it just may not be the right time for that piece to come together in your life. Rest assured that if you attempt to force a piece of the puzzle, somewhere down the road you will have to revisit the placement of that piece and reposition it before you can move forward. When we allow God's will in our lives, the pieces of the puzzle will fit together, just as He intended.

📖 Ephesians 1:9-10 NIV

> ...he made known to us the mystery of his will according to his good pleasure, which he purposed in Christ, to be put into effect when the times reach their fulfillment-to bring unity to all things in heaven and on earth under Christ.

📕 Scriptures to guide your thoughts...

1 Peter 5:10, Job 42:10, Psalm 147:3

🕊 Prayer

Father God, thank you for the pieces of my life that you put together according to your purpose and plan for my life. Amen.

IGNITE

/igˈnīt/

arouse or inflame. (verb)

Unleash Your Power Within

B e stronger than your obstacles, and braver than your fears! You may think that this is easier said than done but know that the Lord has designed you to persevere. Even in times of uncertainty, God has given you the power to forge ahead, not by your strength, but through His. As a believer, you have access to the greatest power, EVER, the Holy Spirit! In fact, the Bible confirms that our bodies are temples of the Holy Spirit which is given by God (1 Corinthians 6:19). Now, take it a step further and think about how often you rely on God's power which has been gifted to you? The interesting part of God's gift is that He gives you the freedom to receive it. In good times, and not so good times, God wants us to trust Him! Have you opened your gift—it's time to unleash your POWER WITHIN!

📖 **Luke 10:19 NIV**

> *I have given you the authority to trample on snakes and scorpions and to overcome all the power of the enemy; nothing will harm you.*

▓ **Scriptures to guide your thoughts...**

2 Samuel 22:23, Job 26:7-14, Romans 15:13, Ephesians 3:20, 2 Corinthians 3:17

🕯 **Prayer**

Lord, I thank you for the power that you have given me. I know that with you by my side I can overcome any obstacle that comes my way. Continue to lead and guide me and continue to show me who I am in you. Amen!

Claim What is Yours

The enemy knows exactly who you are and what gifts you've been blessed with. His goal is to cause you to doubt yourself and question the truth. Don't allow him to make you question what God has already promised you. Furthermore, don't allow the enemy to take it away. When you feel yourself putting a question mark at the end of God's promises, grab it with both hands and yank it into an exclamation mark. Claim what is yours!

📖 **Mark 11:22-24 NIV**

> *"Have faith in God," Jesus answered. Truly I tell you, if anyone says to this mountain, "Go throw yourself into the sea," and does not doubt in their heart but believes that what they say will happen, it will be done for them.*

📕 **Scriptures to guide your thoughts...**

James 4:7, 1 Peter 5:8, 1 Corinthians 10:13

🕯 **Prayer**

Lord, I know what you have promised me, and I will not allow the enemy to use his tricks and schemes to doubt what your Word has already promised. Today, I choose to claim what is mine! Amen.

Stand on God's Promises

A promise is the announcement of an intention and at some point in your life I am sure you've had someone break that intention. However, God is not like man. He stands on His promises. Everything He speaks and everything His word says shall come to pass. Stand on that! Despite what people say and even what you see, remember what He has told you. He will **NEVER** let you down! What God has for you is for you.

📖 Hebrews 10:23 NIV

> *Let us hold unswervingly to the hope we profess, for he who promised is faithful.*

📓 Scriptures to guide your thoughts...

Exodus 14:14, 2 Corinthians 1:20, Joshua 23:14, 2 Peter 3:9

🙏 Prayer

Lord, I thank you for everything you have promised, known or unknown. I will continue to trust you and I will stand on your word. Amen.

Don't Believe the Lies of the Enemy

The only way to recognize a lie is to know the truth and the best way to know the truth is to study the word of God. When the enemy comes, you may not be able outfight him but what you can do is outtruth him so grab your belt of truth and be ready!

Here's some help for you:

When the enemy tells you, "You are weak!" You can fight back with the truth that says, "No! According to Isaiah 40:31, in Him, I am strong."

When the enemy suggests, "You are a failure!" Refute him with the truth that says, "No! According to Romans 8:37, I am more than a conqueror!"

When the enemy tells you, "You are rejected!" You can fight back with the truth that says, "No! According to Ephesians 1:6, in Jesus I am accepted."

When the enemy suggests that, "You are not important!" You can refute him with the truth that says, "No! According to Deuteronomy 7:6, I am God's treasured possession!"

When the enemy tries to convince you that, "Nobody likes you." You can fight back with the truth that says, "No! According to Psalm 17, I am the apple of God's eye."

When the enemy tells you that, "You are a victim!" You can fight back with the truth that says, "No! According to 1 Corinthians 15:57, in Christ, I am victorious."

Next time the enemy tells you that, "You are all alone!" You can refute his lies with the truth that says, "No! According to Joshua 1:5, I am never alone."

When the enemy tries to convince you that, "You are ugly!" You can fight back with the truth that says, "No! According to Psalm 45:11, God says I am beautiful."

When the enemy tells you that, "You are rejected." You refute him with the truth that says, "No! According to 1 John 3:1, God loves me so much He adopted me as His child."

When the enemy tries to discourage you by telling you that "You will never be healed!" You can fight back with the truth that says, "No! According to Isaiah 53:5, by His stripes I am healed."

When the enemy tries to convince you that "You are worthless and unworthy!" You can fight back with the truth that says, "No! According to John 3:16, Jesus declared me worthy!"

📖 Hebrews 4:12 NIV

> *For the word of God is alive and active, sharper than any double-edged sword, it penetrates even to dividing soul and spirit, joints and marrow; it judges the thoughts and attitudes of hearts.*

🕯 Prayer

Lord, thank you for your Word because your Word is my weapon. In Jesus name. Amen.

Yes, You Can!

If you can't remember anything else, remember these three words... Yes, You Can!

How empowering it is when someone says you can't do something and you say, "yes I can!" How motivating is it when every obstacle that comes your way you remember, "yes I can!" How invigorating is it when you are starting a business or changing your career and you say to yourself, "yes I can!" As a believer, you can do all things through Christ! So, remember today and forever, **YES, YOU CAN**!

📖 Matthew 16:19 NIV

> *I will give you the keys of the kingdom of heaven; whatever you bind on earth will be bound in heaven, whatever you loose on earth will be loosed in heaven.*

📓 Scriptures to guide your thoughts...

Philippians 4:13, Matthew 21:22, Mark 11:23, Psalm 27:1, Proverbs 18:21

🕯 Prayer

O' God, how beautiful are the words, "Yes, I Can!" I thank you for giving me the confidence to know that I can do all things. Amen.

God is Greater Than You Could Ever Imagine

Mountains can stop us in our tracks. They can force us to rethink and reevaluate our plans, but have you stopped to think that this is the exact purpose of the mountain? Have your plans taken the place of what God has planned for you? The beauty of the mountain is that it gets our attention and reminds us of our vulnerabilities. God is bigger and He is greater than any mountain you'll encounter! Your weaknesses are no obstacle for God, but in fact opportunities for Him to do His best work. He can use the weakest person if that person relies on Him. Surrender your will to His and watch the mountains move out of your way.

📖 Psalm 147:5

> Greater is our Lord and mighty in power; his understanding has no limit.

▓ Scriptures to guide your thoughts...

Matthew 17:20, Isaiah 54:10, Mark 11:23

✒ Prayer

Heavenly Father know that you are greater than any mountain that tries to stop me in my tracks. You are bigger and you are greater. Amen.

Jesus is the Source

A source is a supplier of something we can't produce on our own but as we have seen, sometimes our sources are subject to shortages depending on the supplier. But not Jesus! He is the source and the supplier, and he provides everything we could ever want or need. Furthermore, he provides a never-ending source for anything we lack a supply of. By coming to HIm and building a relationship with him, you draw the source of all the resources you require. The stock market can go up and down and the economy can change within a blink of an eye but Jesus, he does not change.

📖 **John 14:6-7**

> *Jesus answered, "I am the way and the truth and the life. No one comes to the father except through me. If you really know me, you will know my father as well. From now on, you do know him, and I have seen him."*

📛 **Scriptures to guide your thoughts...**

Philippians 4:19, Psalm 121:1-2, Romans 11:36

✒ **Prayer**

Thank you, Lord, for supplying everything I need. I know that you are my sole source. I will trust you and honor you. Amen.

Heaven is watching and cheering you on!

How blessed are you to have your own cheering squad! When you think no one is cheering for you, remember that you have your own cheering squad in heaven. God knows everything and He sees everything. His eyes run to and from throughout the whole Earth and he doesn't miss a thing. He has faith in you, and he is rooting for you. When you are down and you feel alone, remember that your "squad" is the best one anyone could ever have.

📖 **2 Chronicles 16:9 NIV**

> *For the eyes of the Lord range throughout the earth to strengthen those whose hearts are fully committed to him.*

🔖 **Scriptures to guide your thoughts...**

Jeremiah 33:3, Exodus 14:4, Joshua 23:10, Zephaniah 3:17

🕯 **Prayer**

Heavenly Father, I am grateful to have your team of angels watching over me and cheering me on. My heavenly squad is the best and I thank you! Amen.

The Power of Praise

Have you ever felt like you weren't sure if God was there? Well, here's a "spiritual hack" that you have access to. Did you know that God will occupy the place where His praises are being rendered? The Bible says that God inhabits the praises of his people (Psalm 22:3). When we praise God, our focus shifts from our problems and refocuses our attention on Him. Wonderful things begin to happen when we offer our sacrifice of praise unto God: He delights in our praises (Psalm 149:11); strongholds are destroyed (Psalm 8:2) and the enemy flees (Psalm 34:1). Now that you have been reminded and have knowledge of just how powerful praise is, use it!!

📖 Psalm 150:1-6 NIV

> *"Praise the Lord! Praise God in his sanctuary; praise him in his mighty heavens! Praise him for his mighty deeds; praise him according to his excellent greatness! Praise him with trumpet sound; praise him with lute and harp! Praise him with tambourine and dance; praise him with strings and pipe! Praise him with sounding cymbals; praise him with loud clashing cymbals!*

🕮 Scriptures to guide your thoughts...

Exodus 23:25, Deuteronomy 10:21, 1 Chronicles 16:34, Nehemiah 8:6

✍ Prayer

Heavenly Father I will always give praise to you! I will sing of your greatness and lift up my hands to your Lord because I love you. Amen.

Keep Going, Don't Stop!

Don't allow the opinions of others to stop you from your purpose! In life there will be many naysayers. The enemy himself will even try to deter you but don't let that stop you! Hold true to what you know. Hold true to what you have heard God whisper in your ear. Gain control of your mind and continue to move forward with trust and faith that God has you!

📖 **Matthew 23:9-10 (MSG version)**

> *Don't set people up as experts over your life, letting them tell you what to do. Save that authority for God; let him tell you what to do. No one else should carry the title of 'Father'; you have only one Father, and he's in heaven. And don't let people maneuver you into taking charge of them. There is only one Life-Leader for you and them - Christ.*

📑 **Scriptures to guide your thoughts...**

Galatians 1:10, Proverbs 29:25, Psalm 118:8, 1 Corinthians 1:27

🖋 **Prayer**

Lord, I promise to hold true to the things that you have told me. No longer will I focus on the opinions of others. Your Word is what matters. I will keep going no matter what. Amen.

You Are Destined to Win!

Despite what may be going on in your life, YOU are not losing the battle. God's word says not to be afraid or stressed because the battles aren't ours! Even when it appears that your situation is overtaking you; when you have people coming against you; or when it seems like everything is falling to pieces; remember that *You Are Destined to Win*! You may not always know the reason, but God does--and that is all that matters! If it's a problem or an issue you're dealing with, don't worry! He knew it was going to happen before it happened--and he will help you overcome it.

Remember this, you are Chosen, Appointed, Placed and Purposefully Planted where you're supposed to be!

Destined to win!

📖 1 Corinthians 15:57 NIV

> *But thanks be to God! He gives us the victory through our Lord Jesus Christ.*

🕮 Scriptures to guide your thoughts...

1 John 5:4, Deuteronomy 20:4, 2 Corinthians 4:8-10

📿 Prayer

Lord, thank you for the reminder that the battle is yours not mine. I am a winner, and I am destined to win! Amen.

There is Power in Your Testimony

Break your silence and share what God has done for you. When you share your testimony, it gives others hope. It lets them know that they are not alone. The Bible teaches us on multiple occasions that we should share the Love of God. In doing so, you are not only honoring God by trusting him, but sharing the news with others so that they will come to Him, as well.

📖 **2 Timothy 1:8 NIV**

> *So, do not be ashamed of the testimony about our Lord or of me as his prisoner. Rather, join with me in suffering for the gospel, by the power of God.*

🐛 **Scriptures to guide your thoughts...**

1 Peter 3:15, 1 John 5:9, Luke 21:13

🪶 **Prayer**

Lord, I am grateful for everything I've been through, good or bad and I will not be ashamed to share the goodness of what you have done in my life. Amen.

God's Way is Perfect

God's way is perfect! (Psalm 18-30 KJV) This is a beautiful truth to be grateful for. It may not always be easy; it may not be convenient; it may not come quickly, but we must learn to put our faith and trust in Him. You may have to go over, under, around, or through difficulty—but if you will simply keep your focus on Him, His way, the perfect way, will become yours..

📖 Isaiah 43:19 NIV

> *See, I am doing a new thing! Now it springs up; do you not perceive? I am making a way in the wilderness and streams in the wasteland.*

Scriptures to guide your thoughts…

2 Samuel 22:31, Isaiah 55:8-9, Jeremiah 29:11

🙏 Prayer

God, I know that there is none like you and I choose to go your way. Amen.

NOURISH

/ˈnəriSH/

provide with the food or other
substances necessary for growth. (verb)

Own Your Own Happiness

The ups and downs are an essential part of life just as day and night. However, we cannot allow our dark days to outweigh our light days. Remember, YOU can control your shine. You decide whether you want to be happy and YOU ARE the owner of your happiness button; you can press this button at any time. Don't allow the stressors of this world to keep you in a place of darkness when you can have light. Let your light shine brighter than a diamond and keep pressing that happiness button as if you are pressing a button to win a prize.

📖 1 Thessalonians 5:16-18 NIV

> *Rejoice always, pray continually, give thanks in all circumstances; for this is the will of God in Christ Jesus for you.*

🔖 Scriptures to guide your thoughts...

Romans 15:13, Ecclesiastes 2:26, Proverbs 10:28, Psalm 144:15

🕯 Prayer

Father, today I choose to be happy, and I choose joy. I thank you in advance for my happy days and I thank you for reminding me that I am the owner of happiness even in times of trouble. Amen.

Faith Over Fear

Daily, we are confronted with a multitude of challenges. Unfortunately, these challenges can cause us to feel overwhelmed, discouraged, troubled and ultimately shift our minds to a negative place. But now, more than ever is the time to shift our minds to positive things and renew our way of thinking. There is so much that we can fear and doubt, but God wants us to exercise our faith and overcome our doubts and fears. God never said that we are to live by doubt! He said that we are to live by **FAITH** because without faith, it is impossible to please Him.

📖 Hebrews 10:38 NKJV

> *Now the just shall live by faith; but if any man draws back, my soul shall have no pleasure in him.*

📓 Scriptures to guide your thoughts...

James 1:6, John 11:40, Mark 10:52, Luke 1:37

✍ Prayer

Father, help me to replace my fears with faith. Help me to remember that with only a mustard seed of faith I can move mountains. Shift my thinking and remove any doubt. Amen.

Put Your Pride Aside!

Be obsessed with wanting to improve yourself and do this by seeking help! You cannot do everything on your own. The Lord didn't make us that way. He made us to be a community. He made us to depend on each other. He made us to support each other and build each other up. God will put people in your life specifically to help you in the areas in which you lack but if you don't ask, you won't receive.

📖 James 4:2 NIV

> *You desire and you do not have, so you kill. You covet and cannot get what you want, so you fight and quarrel. You do not have, because you do not ask.*

▆ Scriptures to guide your thoughts...

Proverbs 11:2, Proverbs 16:5, Obadiah 1:3

🕊 Prayer

Lord, please forgive me for my pride. Today, I choose to put my pride aside. I understand that I cannot always do things on my own and I thank you for those who are here to help me. Amen.

Stop Doubting Yourself

Why am I not good enough? This is a question that has crossed the minds of many at one point or another. Even the most confident person has experienced times when they wonder why someone didn't recognize their worth. But remember, don't let anyone or anything make you feel less than you are because YOU ARE GOOD ENOUGH, and YOU ARE WORTHY. Even in your weakest moments, do not allow the tricks of the enemy to steer you away from what God has said in his Word about you! Meditate on the Word and know the TRUTH!

📖 **1 Peter 2:9 NIV**

> *But you are a chosen people, a royal priesthood, a holy nation, God's special possession, that you may declare the praises of him who called you out of darkness into his wonderful light.*

🔥 **Scriptures to guide your thoughts...**

Mark 9:21-24, John 20:24-29, James 1:6

🕯 **Prayer**

Dear God, thank you for reminding me that I AM ENOUGH! No longer will I doubt myself or let anyone else doubt me. I know what I am worth, and I know that I am all you have called me to be. Amen.

Rejection is Not Always Bad

Rejection is definitely one of those things that can make us feel unworthy, unwanted and unqualified. However, when a door closes in your life, it does not always equate to something bad. Sometimes God allows a door to be closed to protect us or it could be a redirection. It may also mean it's time to move on. So don't get upset or weary when a door closes, rather, thank God for keeping you safe and know in your heart that He has something greater in store for you. A closed door is not always a locked door!

📖 Revelation 3:7 NIV

> To the angel of the church in Philadelphia write:
> These are the words of Him who is holy and true, who
> holds the key of David. What He opens no one can shut,
> and what he shuts no one can open.

📓 Scriptures to guide your thoughts...

Hebrews 10:35, Matthew 7:7, Romans 8:28

🙏 Prayer

Father God, although rejection doesn't feel good, I thank you for the closed doors because the closed doors mean it wasn't for me in the first place. Thank you for knowing what's best. Amen.

Focus on God, Not Your Problems!

The more you focus on a problem, the more you magnify it!

Sometimes it is easy to overlook the simple things in life because we focus more on our situation versus the faithfulness of God. Additionally, we get so caught up on what we don't have, and we lose sight of all the wonderful blessings that surround us. When we live by faith, we believe God has everything under control and it shows in our thoughts, words and actions. Remember, that worrying doesn't change anything but trusting God changes everything! Also, start practicing a routine of gratefulness and as Ephesians 5:20 reminds us...

Give thanks to God the Father for everything, in the name of our Lord Jesus Christ.

🔖 **Scriptures to guide your thoughts...**

Philippians 4:6, Psalm 46:10, Hebrews 3:1, Proverbs 5: 1-2

🕯 **Prayer**

Lord, I thank you. No longer will I focus on my problems, but I will focus on you. I am grateful for the good and the bad. Amen.

How Will You Use Your Gifts?

God has given us certain gifts and talents; however, it is up to us to tap into those gifts and talents and make use of them. Often, we get caught up on feeling incapable and we lose our focus. Redirect your focus and exercise your God given gifts and talents so that you can strengthen them and live out the purpose that God has for your life.

📖 **1 Peter 4:10 NIV**

> *Each of you should use whatever gift you have received to serve others, as faithful stewards of God's grace in its various forms.*

📓 **Scriptures to guide your thoughts...**

1 Corinthians 12:4-6, James 1:17, Ephesians 2:10, Matthew 25:14, Proverbs 18:16

🕯 **Prayer**

Heavenly Father, I thank you for the many gifts that you have blessed me with and Lord even though I may not know what they all are now. I promise that I will make good use of them. Amen.

Silence is Golden

To truly hear from God, sometimes we must unplug from all the noise and clutter in our lives. It may be difficult due to the multiple responsibilities we have but hearing from God is essential.

Also, we must learn that when we don't hear God, it may be because he wants us to do what we already know to do or if He has already given us instructions, we are to follow the instructions previously given. Furthermore, when God is quiet, know that he is always watching and working behind the scenes. Trust His presence.

📖 Psalm 37:7 NIV

> *Be still before the Lord and wait patiently for Him...*

📣 Scriptures to guide your thoughts...

Isaiah 65:24, Psalm 13, Romans 12:12

🕊 Prayer

Lord, I understand that just because I don't hear from you doesn't mean you aren't there. Thank you for your silence and trusting me to do what I need to do. Amen.

What are You Sacrificing?

For God so loved the world that He gave His only begotten son. The ultimate sacrifice! So, I ask you, what are you sacrificing for Him? God calls us to turn away from sin and live a life that is pleasing to him but often we find difficulty in that, why? I encourage you to think about how Jesus died on the cross. Remember all that He endured and then when those desires of the flesh tempt you, think and ask yourself, "Is it worth it?"

📖 **Romans 6:13 NIV**

> *Do not offer any part of yourself to sin as an instrument of wickedness, but rather offer yourselves to God as those who have been brought from death to life; and offer every part of yourself to him as an instrument of righteousness.*

▓ **Scriptures to guide your thoughts...**

John 14:15, 1 John 5:17, 1 John 3:4

🕊 **Prayer**

Lord, thank you for the ultimate sacrifice, your son, Jesus. I pray that you help me to resist the desires of my flesh because it's not worth it. In your name I pray, Amen.

Choose Your Words Wisely

As we have seen spoken about in the Bible, there is power in your tongue, so choose your words wisely. Be careful how you speak and be mindful of the things you say. You have the choice to either tear down and destroy or build up and be life giving. Which do you choose?

If we understood the power of our thoughts, we would guard them more closely. If we understood the power of our words, we would prefer silence to anything negative. In our thoughts and words, we create our own weaknesses and our own strengths. Our limitations and joys begin in our hearts. We can always replace negative with positive. ~ Betty Eadie

📖 Psalm 141:3 NIV

> *Set a guard over my mouth, Lord; keep a watch over the doors of my lips.*

📑 Scriptures to guide your thoughts...

Matthew 12:37, Ephesians 4:29, Proverbs 18:21, Proverbs 12:6,

🙏 Prayer

Lord, let my words be a reflection of who you say I am. Let me also be reminded that life and death are in the power of the tongue and what I speak, I call into being. I will choose my words wisely. Amen.

God's Timing

Remember that the right timing is God's timing. We sometimes get so consumed with the world's timeline or what we see others doing that we forget that God is all-knowing and that He knows what is best for us. Don't allow what you see happening in the world determine what should be your destiny.

📖 **2 Peter 3:8-9 NIV**

> *But do not forget this one thing, dear friends: With the Lord, a day is like a thousand years, and a thousand years are like a day. The Lord is not slow in keeping his promise, as some understand slowness. Instead, He is patient with you, not wanting everyone to perish, but everyone to come to repentance*

▓ **Scriptures to guide your thoughts...**

Proverbs 16:9, Proverbs 27:1, Lamentations 3:25-26, Habakkuk 2:3, Psalm 27:14, Galatians 1:19

📿 **Prayer**

Lord, I will wait on you. I understand that your time is the best time because good things come to those who wait. Amen.

EDIFY

/ˈedəˌfī/

improve (someone) morally or intellectually. (verb)

Check Your Circle

You cannot win when you have people around you who drain you of your energy. So, when you ask yourself, "Why am I not where I need to be?" Look around and pay attention to the people you surround yourself with. If you are not surrounded by people who encourage you, motivate you and support you then it is time to change your circle. Misery loves company and the longer you stay in a toxic and negative circle, the more you give misery and negativity the opportunity to overcome you.

📖 **Proverbs 13:20 NKJV**

> *Whoever walks with the wise becomes wise, but the companion of fools will be destroyed.*

📖 **1 Corinthians 15:33 NIV**

> *Do not be deceived: "Evil company corrupts good habits."*

📖 **Scriptures to guide your thoughts...**

2 Corinthians 6:14, Matthew 5:30, Proverbs 14:7, Psalm 1:1, Proverbs 22:24-25

🙏 **Prayer**

Lord, help me to recognize the energy of those around me. Open my eyes and give me the courage to remove myself from those who aren't good for me. Amen.

Give Thanks

Giving thanks is so important to being able to hear God's voice because, like praise and worship, it is something God responds to.

I encourage you to examine your life, pay attention to your thoughts and your words, and see how much gratitude you express. In fact, try to get through an entire day without one complaint. Develop an attitude of gratitude in every situation. In fact, just become overly thankful - and watch; your relationship with God will increase and He will pour out even more blessings than ever before.

📖 1 Thessalonians 5:18 NIV

Give thanks in all circumstances; for this is the will of God in Christ Jesus for you.

📖 Scriptures to guide your thoughts...

Chronicles 16:34, Colossians 4:2, Psalm 50:14, Proverbs 18:20

🕯 Prayer

Father, I thank you for everything that you have done, you are doing and will do. Amen.

Pursue God for Who He Is

Pursue God for His "presence." In other words, pursue God for who He is, not for what He can do for you. Making your requests known to God is definitely what we should do, however, sometimes He just wants us to converse with Him without asking for anything. We shouldn't go to him *only* when we need or want something.

When you're in constant communication with Him, you'll experience a relationship that soothes your soul. You'll experience walking in His will. Furthermore, you'll also see that wishes don't always come true, but prayers often do.

📖 Deuteronomy 4:29 NIV

> *But if from there you seek the Lord your God, you will find Him if you seek Him with all your heart and with all your soul.*

📓 Scriptures to guide your thoughts...

Mark 10:27, 2 John 1:9, Revelation 3:20, James 4:8

🙏 Prayer

Lord, please forgive me for the times I've come to you only with requests. I do desire to have a real relationship with you and I thank you for blessing me even when sometimes I didn't deserve it. Amen.

God Works on His Time, Not Ours

Unfortunately, we live in a world where everything is "right now." Everyone wants the quick fix or the easy way out. They want to see the end result without putting in the necessary work, but God is not a "right now," God. One of the most crucial lessons we must learn is practicing patience. God is not in a hurry so why should you be?

📖 **Romans 8:25 NIV**

> *But if we hope for what we do not yet have, we wait for it patiently.*

📓 **Scriptures to guide your thoughts...**

> *Proverbs 14:29, Galatians 6:9, Psalm 37:7, Exodus 14:14*

🙏 **Prayer**

Lord, I pray that you help me understand that good things come to those who wait and although I'm anxious to know what the future holds, I trust YOU! Amen.

God is Working it Out

Many times, we try to do things on our own and when it doesn't work, we get frustrated and start soliciting help from other people instead of relying and trusting in God. Yes, I know things get hard, and yes things get challenging, but when God steps in with his strategy, which he's already designed for your life, he comes in and works it all out and puts it together like the pieces of the puzzle.

So as a reminder even though your life may look chaotic right now, or it looks like things are not coming together, remember that God is in the background working it out for you! He is moving pieces together and aligning them according to his plan. Continue to do your part and he'll put your life together just as the pieces of a puzzle were put together.

📖 John 5:17 NIV

> *In his defense Jesus said to them, "My Father is always at work to this very day, and I too am working."*

📕 Scriptures to guide your thoughts...

1 Corinthians 10:13, Romans 8:28, Philippians 1:6

🙏 Prayer

Lord, thank you for working things out for me. Even though my life looks chaotic right now, I have faith that you will work everything out. Amen.

Change Your Words

You must speak your dreams into existence. And more than just speaking them, you must BELIEVE and TRUST those blessings are coming.

Instead of saying: "I don't know how to do it,"

Say: "I am committed to LEARN how to do it."

Instead of saying: "I'm a failure,"

Say: "I've failed, I've learned the lesson and WHEN I become a huge success that failure is going to make an awesome story."

Instead of believing others are born lucky or with special gifts – KNOW that YOU ARE capable of anything!

📖 Proverbs 18:4 ESV

> *A person's words can be life-giving water; words of true wisdom are as refreshing as a bubbling brook.*

📓 Scriptures to guide your thoughts...

Proverbs 12:18, Proverbs 15:4, Colossians 4:6,

✒ Prayer

Father, I trust, believe and have faith in everything your word promises me. Amen.

Are You Ready for Combat?

Let's armor up! The war of good versus evil is a fight we come against every day! As we know, the enemy comes to steal, kill and destroy. He is motivated by evil and tries to stir up hate and will not stop until what is good is destroyed.

Fortunately, our God Almighty has equipped us with everything we need to fight the battle and win the war so we must use the tools he has given us.

📖 **Ephesians 6:11-12 NIV**

> *Put on the full armor of God, so that you can take your stand against the devil's schemes.* ¹² *For our struggle is not against flesh and blood, but against the rulers, against the authorities, against the powers of this dark world and against the spiritual forces of evil in the heavenly realms.*

🦋 **Scriptures to guide your thoughts...**

1 Peter 5:8, Matthew 12:25, 2 Chronicles 25:8

🕯 **Prayer**

Lord, thank you for equipping me with the tools I need to fight the enemy. He has no power, and I will continue to fight with everything I have in me. Amen

God's Time = Perfect Timing

We as human beings want things to happen at the "perfect time," but what is the perfect time? Unfortunately, things may not always happen when we want them and when they don't, we get discouraged, but remember, God's time is ALWAYS the perfect time. He knows what we can handle, and He knows what is best for us so next time something doesn't happen when you want it to, just know that God has your best interest at heart and say to yourself, Ok God, I know; not my time but your time."

Ecclesiastes 3:11 NNIV

He has made everything beautiful in its time. He has also set eternity in the human heart; yet no one can fathom what God has done from beginning to end.

Scriptures to guide your thoughts...

Habakkuk 2:3, Lamentations 3:25-26, Isaiah 40:31

Prayer

Heavenly Father please help me to be patient. Although we live in a "right now world" I know that your time is always the perfect time.

Spend Quality Time
With God

Take time to pray and have a simple conversation with God. This pleases him and it gives honor to Him. You may even ask God, "What do you want to do in and through me?" versus asking Him what you want Him to do for you. This question will help you discover what is truly meant for you versus what you think you should be doing because of what other people are doing.

📖 1 Chronicles 16:11 NIV

> *Look to the Lord and his strength; seek his face always.*

📓 Scriptures to guide your thoughts...

Matthew 6:6, 1 Chronicles 16:11, James 4:8

🙏 Prayer

Lord, I thank you for the opportunity to build a relationship with you and I know that I can only do this by spending quality time. You are always here Lord God and I thank you for that. Amen.

Will You Answer the Call?

Before you were even born, God had an assignment and a unique purpose for your life. He knew every detail about you, every gift and talent you would possess, and the steps he would strategically orchestrate for you. However, you still have a responsibility to be willing to accept the plan and purpose that God has for you.

Often, God will push us into what we are called to do, but other times he won't because he gives us the ability to make choices. He is calling you to lead a specific charge and wants you to exemplify the qualities that mirror Him. Will you answer the call? Will you be open to truly living out your God-given purpose, your assignment? If so, he is waiting. You have exactly what you need inside of you. You just have to be open and willing. God makes no mistakes, and even when you don't recognize your greatness, He does!

📖 Matthew 5:16 NIV

> *In the same way, let your light shine before others, that they may see your good deeds and glorify your Father in heaven.*

📓 Scriptures to guide your thoughts...

Ephesians 1:11, Proverbs 2:9, Psalm 16:5

🙏 Prayer

Lord, thank you for my purpose. I know you have destined me for greatness and even when I don't feel it, I trust you. Amen!

Victory is Yours!

"Victory is mine, victory is mine, victory today is mine. I told Satan, get thee behind, victory today is mine." Oh, how I love this song. This song gives great encouragement. However, where there is victory, struggle may also come. Jesus wants us to understand that there will be days and even seasons of life that are incredibly difficult. Scripture never promises that faith in Jesus will make our problems go away but at the end of the day we will prevail, and victory will indeed be ours. Stay the course!

📖 **1 John 5:4 NIV**

> *...for everyone born of God overcomes the world. This is the victory that has overcome the world, even our faith.*

🎗 **Scriptures to guide your thoughts...**

> *Deuteronomy 20:4, 1 Corinthians 15:57, 1 Chronicles 29:11, Exodus 15:1*

🕊 **Prayer**

Lord, despite the struggles, I thank you in advance for the victory. In Jesus' name. Amen!

Eliminate the Distractions

It is important that we keep our focus on God and eliminate any and all distractions. With so many things at our fingertips such as social media, it is easy for us to shift our minds to earthly things versus things up above. During your time dedicated to God, that should be the focus. Turn off the notifications, clear your mind and even put your phone on do not disturb if you have to so that you can give Him the time he deserves.

📖 1 Corinthians 7:35 ESV

> *I say this for your own benefit, not to lay any restraint upon you, but to promote good order and to secure your undivided devotion to the Lord.*

📑 Scriptures to guide your thoughts...

2 Timothy 2:15, Colossians 3:1, Matthew 6:24, Hebrews 12:1-2

🙏 Prayer

Lord, I thank you for the time and attention that you give me, and I promise to do the same. Amen.

When God Sees Your Faithfulness

I know it may seem like your storm will never end but your storm won't last forever. Good things are coming your way! Continue to trust Him and don't give up. Keep persevering! His Favor is yours. His provision belongs to you. His blessings are stored up for you. His plan for your life is in motion. Lift your head to the sky. Stay encouraged. God will honor your faithfulness!

📖 Matthew 25:23 NIV

> *His lord said unto him, 'Well done, good and faithful servant. You have been faithful and trustworthy over a little, I will put you in charge of many things. Come and share your master's happiness.*

📓 Scriptures to guide your thoughts...

Samuel 26:23, Revelation 2:10, James 1:12 - 22

📖 Prayer

Lord, I know my troubles won't last forever. I thank you for the reminder. Please give me the strength to carry on. In Jesus name, Amen.

Final Words

YOU MADE IT! How do you feel? I hope that you feel blessed, and I hope you are encouraged! God's Word is real and as you hopefully have seen by the messages in this book, there is a scripture that can apply to any area of your life. Use them! And remember what God says about you. He loves you and he wants a relationship with you. He wants to bless you so allow him to do that. Be encouraged and God Bless!

📖 **Numbers 6:24-26**

> *May the Lord bless you and keep you; may the Lord make his face shine upon you and be gracious unto you; and may the Lord lift his countenance upon you and give you peace.*

ACKNOWLEDGMENTS

*Trying to write a book when you spend so much time helping others write theirs is truly a challenge. For so long I've put this book on the back burner because I just didn't have the time, but God said, "It is time!" Thankfully, I had my dear sorority sister, Chanda Carey-Vickerstaff constantly reminding me that it **IS** my time and it's time to stop hiding. Sis, you have encouraged me more than you know, and I truly appreciate you for staying on me and encouraging me to do what God has called me to do.*

To my Aunt Cheryl, thank you for always encouraging me and supporting me. I love you!

Daddy, I love you! I am just trying to make you proud!

To my best-friend Leah Nicholson. You are always there! You support me in everything I do. Whatever I need, I know that you have my back 110%.

To my very good friend Chris Mayweather, words cannot even begin to express how grateful and appreciative I am of you. I will forever treasure our friendship.

Finally, to all those who have been a part of me finally getting here, family and friends, whether you knew it or not, thank you! Laweisha Loggins, Cindy Bragg, Dynette Davis, Brandon Crosby. God is about to take us all higher than we could ever imagine! Thank you for your support!

ABOUT THE AUTHOR

Eydie Robinson is an International Best-Selling author, motivational speaker, the Founder of Desire to Empower, a non-profit 501c3 organization, Owner of Robinson Anderson Publishing LLC., and most important a lover of the Lord. She resides in Dallas, TX and is the mother of three children.

Eydie has written several books and journals and has been a part of various collaborations: *Life Behind Closed Doors, Women Inspiring Nations, Voices of the 21st Century, Marriage and the Aftermath, Change Your Words, Transform Your Life* and *From Passion to Published.*

Eydie is a proud member of Alpha Kappa Alpha Sorority, Incorporated where she serves as Chaplain for the Omega Alpha Omega chapter in Frisco, TX.

To learn more about Eydie go to:

www.eydierobinson.com

IG: @theonlyeydierobinson

FB: @theonlyeydierobinson

CPSIA information can be obtained
at www.ICGtesting.com
Printed in the USA
BVHW040946250822
645501BV00002B/52